T

# Purifying Modern Christianity Through the Original Demands of Jesus and His Apostles

JESUS PRAYED FOR YOU:
" Neither pray I for these alone (APOSTLES), but for them also (You) which shall believe on me through their (APOSTLES) word.
JOHN 17:20

By
Darin Bowler

What you believe is very important.   I TIMOTHY 4:16

Note for Librarians: A cataloguing record for this book is available from Library and Archives Canada at www.collectionscanada.ca/amicus/index-e.html Printed in Victoria, BC, Canada.

ISBN: 9781453732717

Order copies at www.createspace.com/3473162

To Mom and Jerry

"If ye believe not that I am he, ye shall die in your sins" – Jesus

"He that believeth and is baptized shall be saved; but he that believeth not shall be damned." – Jesus

"Except ye repent, ye shall all likewise perish." – Jesus

"So then they that are in the flesh cannot please God. But ye are not in the flesh, but in the Spirit, if so be that the Spirit of God dwell in you. Now if any man have not the Spirit of Christ, he is none of his." - St. Paul

"The Lord Jesus shall be revealed from heaven with his mighty angels, in flaming fire taking vengeance on them that know not God, and that obey not the gospel of our Lord Jesus Christ." - St. Paul

# Contents

# Chapter One

## Partial Faith Syndrome

Once upon a time there was a very wealthy man who passed away, apparently without leaving a will. According to the law his estate was to be divided amongst his only surviving distant relatives. Also all of his household goods were to be converted into cash at a public auction. During the sale the auctioneer held up a framed photograph of the deceased man's son, but no one bid on it. Not even the relatives that were present. After the auction a woman approached the auctioneer and asked if she could purchase the photograph for a dollar. She explained that she was a servant in the man's house and that the boy had died many years ago. The auctioneer accepted the dollar and the woman took the photograph home and placed it on a table beside her bed. At that moment she noticed a slight bulge in the back of the frame. She undid the backing and there she found the rich man's will. The instructions were very simple. It read, "I give and bequeath all of my properties and possessions to the person who cares enough for my son to own and cherish this photograph." So the woman became the heir of all that the man possessed.[1]

In one sense God is very much the same as this man. Obviously this man was not content to allow just anyone to inherit his possessions. The heir needed to be someone who at least showed an interest in that which he cherished and loved the most—his son. In one sense God is very much the same way. The truth is, not everyone is going to be saved. Not everyone is going to inherit eternal life in heaven.

**Then said one unto him, Lord, are there few that be saved? And he said unto them, Strive to enter in at the strait gate: for many, I say unto you, will seek to enter in, and shall not be able (Luke 13:23-24).**

If anyone is going to be saved it will be those who manifested an active interest in discovering what was pleasing to God and what His will actually was. The saved are going to be numbered amongst those who valued and loved the things that God valued and loved. It will be those who sought to serve Him and obey His will. But how do we really know or discover what God's will is? What is the means by which He has chosen to reveal Himself and His will to us? Well, there are basically two ways that God has chosen to reveal Himself to the human race. The first means of revelation is within the creation around us.

**The heavens declare the glory of God; and the firmament sheweth his handywork. Day unto day uttereth speech, and night unto night sheweth knowledge. There is no speech nor language, where their voice is not heard (Psalm 19:1-3).**

In other words, it doesn't matter what language one speaks or what part of the world one lives in, all one has to do is look around to observe the fact that there is a God. Nature constantly proclaims that reality.

The second means that God has chosen to reveal Himself to humanity is through His Word, the Bible. Now the creation is only a *general* revelation of Himself, but His Word is a much more *specific* revelation. The creation helps us to know that there is a God, but His Word actually tells us who He is. His Word tells us how to worship Him and how to serve Him. His Word tells us what He likes and what He dislikes, what is acceptable and what is not acceptable. Remember, not just anyone and everyone is going to be saved. It's going to be those who showed an active interest in discovering what was pleasing to Him and what His will was. Now, Jesus once said, "Ye do err not knowing the scriptures" (Matthew 22:29). In other words, you're making a serious mistake or doing wrong (error) by not familiarizing yourself in detail with what the scriptures actually say. In John 5:39 He said, "Search the scriptures…these are they which testify of me." If one really wants to know the details of who God is and what He is about, one needs to familiarize himself with the Bible. The most important and profound truths of all time, space and matter are contained within its pages.

Now this may surprise you, but the most precious commodity in the world is not gold. It is not oil and it is not diamonds either. The absolutely most precious commodity in all existence is **Truth.** Now, in one sense truth is very much *like* gold, oil and diamonds in the fact that it is not commonly found just anywhere and everywhere in plain open sight. For instance, you don't take a stroll down your sidewalk in the evenings to find gold lying in the gutters or on your neighbor's lawn or in the street. You don't find diamonds in your cereal box. Well, just as the most precious commodities of the earth are buried deep beneath the soil, so also is truth buried deep within the pages of the Bible. And truth is of much greater value than any material wealth:

**The law of the LORD is perfect, converting the soul: The testimony of the LORD is sure, making wise the simple. The statutes of the LORD are right, rejoicing the heart: The commandment of the LORD is pure, enlightening the eyes. The fear of the LORD is clean, enduring forever: The judgments of the LORD are true and righteous altogether. More to be desired are they than gold, yea, than much fine gold: sweeter also than honey and the honeycomb. Moreover by them is thy servant warned: and in keeping of them there is great reward (Psalm 19:7-11).**

This fact that truth is often "buried" out of plain sight is further observed in the Book of Isaiah. Notice these words very carefully:

**But the word of the LORD was unto them precept upon precept, precept upon precept; line upon line, line upon line; here a little, and there a little; that they might go, and fall backward, and be broken, and snared, and taken (Isaiah 28:13).**

Now, we have to ask ourselves this question: "How is it that God's Word given line upon line, precept upon precept, here a little and there a little can actually cause people to *fall,* become *broken, snared* and *taken*? Isn't God's Word supposed to keep us from these travesties?" Well, the Word of God is deliberately "sprinkled" or interwoven throughout with very precious nuggets of truth. Here a little and there a little. It is intentionally and deliberately structured that way so that only the sincerely interested and curious will seek and discover truth. The uninterested won't. Remember, truth is much like gold. It is very valuable and one has to search for it. That's one reason why Jesus likened a true and wise disciple to a man who "dug deep" and found a sure and solid foundation upon which to build his house.

**And why call ye me, Lord, Lord, and do not the things which I say? Whosoever cometh to me, and heareth my sayings, and doeth them. I will shew you to whom he is like: he is like a man which built a house, and digged deep, and laid the foundation on a rock: and when the flood arose, the stream beat vehemently upon that house, and could not shake it: for it was founded upon a rock. But he that heareth, and doeth not, is like a man that without a foundation built an house upon the**

**earth; against which the stream did beat vehemently, and immediately it fell; and the ruin of that house was great (Luke 6:46-49).**

Now, the problem with many people today and even a lot of "Christians" is that they don't "dig deep." With only a casual familiarity with only the more "popular" passages of scripture they develop only a partial familiarity with truth. They too quickly formulate decisions and jump to conclusions without carefully considering more of what the Bible has to say about particular subjects. They suffer with a little problem that we'll just call Partial Faith Syndrome. Sadly, however, the consequences of Partial Faith Syndrome can be of a spiritual and an eternal nature. Remember, Jesus said, "Ye do err not knowing the scriptures." Now just in case you think that Partial Faith Syndrome is not a reality to be concerned with, let's quickly consider one biblical event that demonstrates Partial Faith Syndrome in action. Did you know that it was always promised and prophesied deep within the ancient writings of the Old Testament that God would one day reveal or manifest Himself as a man? Somewhere around 740 B.C. the prophet Isaiah penned these words:

**For unto us a child is born, unto us a son is given... and his name shall be called Wonderful, Counseller, The mighty God, The everlasting Father, The Prince of Peace (Isaiah 9:6).**

Did you get that? This Son, this Child would in fact be God Himself. Around 600 B.C. the prophet Jeremiah also shed some light on this amazing promise:

**Behold, the days come, saith the LORD, that I will raise unto David a righteous Branch, and a King shall reign and prosper, and shall execute judgment and justice in the earth. In his days Judah shall be saved, and Israel shall dwell safely: and this is his name whereby he shall be called, THE LORD OUR RIGHTEOUSNESS (Jeremiah 23:5-6).**

Wow, what an amazing promise! Some day God is going to raise up a physical descendant of King David himself. This king will prosper and execute judgment and justice throughout the entire world! In his days the land of Israel will dwell in safety. And his name whereby he shall be called is none other than...THE LORD OUR RIGHTEOUSNESS. This King is going to be God Himself! You see, it was always prophesied that God would one day manifest Himself as a man. Yet somehow *through time* that precious truth slowly became neglected, lost and mostly forgotten by many of God's people. Why, it was even prophesied precisely when He would actually show up (see Daniel 9:25). But again, somehow *through time* this precious truth became neglected and dismissed. And it was precisely this ignorance that Jesus was addressing when He said these words:

**And he said also to the people, when ye see a cloud rise out of the west, straightway ye say, there cometh a shower, and so it is. And when ye see the south wind blow, ye say, There will be heat; and it cometh to pass. Ye hypocrites, ye can discern the face of the sky and of the earth; but how is it that ye do not discern this time? (Luke 12:54-56).**

In essence He was saying, "If you would just go to the writings of the prophets and 'do your homework,' you would know who is standing in front of you right now." It is very interesting to me how some people seem to be more interested in Jesus' skin color than they are in what He actually had to say. Many it seems are eager to identify with Him on some level but yet at the same time they blatantly disregard and ignore who He actually is. Keep in mind that Jesus Himself said things like "He that hath seen me hath seen the Father" (John 14:9). He also said, "If ye believe not that I am he, ye shall die in your sins" (John 8:24). But many of the people in Jesus' day were guilty of Partial Faith Syndrome. Partial Faith Syndrome in its purest form is when you really do believe *in* God, but you really don't *believe* God. And such is the case with a lot of people today. Sadly, such is the case with even a lot of "Christians" today. Somehow through time the original teachings of Jesus and the apostles have gradually been reduced to an inferior, secondary source of knowledge and truth. Somehow *through time* the theological and doctrinal teachings of ordinary men have been embraced and exalted *more* than the first and original teachings of Jesus and the apostles.

Now, before we go any further in this discourse it is absolutely imperative that we first understand *why* the teachings of the apostles are of such importance and in fact as equally authoritative as the teachings of Jesus Himself. First notice what Jesus Himself once told His disciples:

**But the Comforter, which is the Holy Ghost, whom the Father will send in my name, he shall teach you all things and bring all things to your remembrance, whatsoever I have said unto you (John 14:26).**

Did you get that? (I'll tell on myself). Sometimes I have a hard time remembering what my wife said just a few minutes earlier. So this passage is even more impressive to me. But the disciples were supernaturally empowered to remember *everything* Jesus ever said to them. Notice this passage also. Jesus is still talking to His disciples:

**Howbeit when he, the Spirit of truth is come, he will guide you into all truth (John 16:13).**

This is how the apostles got the authority to teach the things that they taught. They were personally led by the Spirit of God into *all* truth. And they were supernaturally empowered to remember *everything* Jesus ever said to them. They didn't just make this stuff up! This is precisely why our doctrine should not differ from that of the apostles. The teachings of Jesus and the apostles are the only truly solid and perfectly accurate foundation upon which to build.

**Now therefore ye are no more strangers and foreigners, but fellowcitizens with the saints, and of the household of God; and are built upon the foundation of the apostles and prophets, Jesus Christ himself being the chief cornerstone (Ephesians 2:19-20).**

So we see then that we are not built upon the teachings of ordinary men that lived and came upon the scene years *after* Jesus and the apostles. We are not built upon Justin Martyr, Martin Luther, Charles Russell or Joseph Smith. We are not built upon Max Lucado, Joel Osteen, Rick Warren or Billy Graham. We are not built upon the pope, your pastor or my pastor. True Christianity, in its purest form, is built upon the original teachings of Jesus and the apostles. True Christians endeavor to practice, apply and obey the original commands of Jesus and the apostles no matter how unpopular those commands may ever become or how much they may alienate them from the majority of everyone else in the world. And let me warn you. If you choose to seriously live by the original teachings of Jesus and His apostles it most certainly will separate you from the majority. And sadly that's a price many people don't want to pay. But it's absolutely imperative that we hold to the same relentless, undying confidence in the certainty of God's Word that the Apostle Paul held to:

**Let God be true, but every man a liar (Romans 3:4).**

This same attitude of absolute, undying faith in the Scriptures is the first essential step in order to be truly rooted and firmly established in pure, authentic Christianity. This will serve as the only remedy to annihilate a terminal case of Partial Faith Syndrome.

# Chapter Two

## Doctrinal Malnutrition

There once was an old farmer who found an eagle's egg and placed it in the nest of a chicken. Eventually the eaglet hatched with the brood of chicks and grew up right along with them. The eagle, thinking he was a chicken, did just exactly what the chickens did. He clucked and cackled. He flew in only a brief thrashing of wings and flurry of feathers no more than a few feet off the ground. After all, that's how chickens were supposed to fly. He never knew what it was to taste the healthy, nourishing and satisfying kill of a duck, rabbit or a fresh salmon. Instead he scratched in the dirt for seeds and insects to eat. Naturally he was a bit thin and considerably malnourished. Years passed and the eagle grew very old. One day he saw a magnificent bird soaring far above him in the cloudless sky. Hanging with graceful majesty on the powerful currents of wind, it soared with scarcely a beat of its strong healthy wings. "What a magnificent bird!" said the eagle. "What is it?" "Why, that's an eagle—the king of the birds," a chicken clucked. "But don't give it a second thought. You could never be like him." So the eagle never gave it another thought. And he died thinking he was a chicken.[1]

How sad it is that there are many people just like that eagle. People who never really reach their full potential or purpose in life because of the negative environments that surround them. Brilliant children who truly believe that they are stupid and destined to fail because of the hurtful, insulting and damaging remarks of unwise parents. People who never dare to dream or achieve anything just because of the small thinking nay-sayers that compass them daily. People who plan the course of their lives only according to the patterns of their immediate environments. What a vicious and dismal cycle of hopelessness that is created when people only believe what they are told to believe.

It is even more tragic in a spiritual parallel when we consider the untold thousands of souls who routinely believe whatever they are told. People who never take the time to inform themselves in detail of what Jesus and the apostles actually said.

The problem we observed in the previous chapter was essentially a lack of *faith* in God's Word. The problem we'll now observe is essentially centered on a lack of *knowledge* of God's Word. An ignorance of what the Bible actually has to say about a few things. President Lyndon B. Johnson once said, "Poverty has many roots, but the tap root is ignorance." [2] God put it this way:

**My people are destroyed for lack of knowledge (Hosea 4:6).**

Notice a certain prophecy that was written some two thousand years ago that is now being fulfilled today:

**For the time will come when they shall not endure sound doctrine; but after their own lusts shall they heap to themselves teachers, having itching ears; And they shall turn away their ears from the truth, and shall be turned unto fables (II Timothy 4:3-4).**

Obviously the Apostle Paul foresaw a day when "Christians" would not endure (remain with) sound doctrine. In other words they wouldn't stick with the original doctrine. He foresaw a day when the teachings of the apostles would be mentally set aside in favor of "new and improved" teachings. The Apostle Peter also foresaw this coming trend:

**But there were false prophets also among the people, even as there shall be false teachers among you…and many shall follow their pernicious ways by reason of whom the way of truth shall be evil spoken of (II Peter 2:1-2).**

Peter foresaw a day when the truth would actually be called evil by certain teachers. While claiming to be Christians they would still have the bold audacity to teach and speak things that diametrically oppose the things that the apostles taught. By doing this they would in reality be denying Jesus Himself. Then they would go so far as to label the way of truth as evil. And not just a few but *many* would follow their foolish and destructive ways. The apostles foresaw a day when innumerable masses of individuals would be misled by the teachings of men. When people would be spiritually ruined through a lack of knowledge. This is a problem that we'll just call "Doctrinal Malnutrition."

Now allow me to be technical for just a moment. The first prophecy that we looked at in this chapter (II Timothy 4:3-4) holds an even greater significance to pastors or Bible teachers. The reason being that II Timothy is known as a "pastoral epistle." That's a fancy way of saying it was a letter sent to a pastor. II Timothy was a letter of divine instruction from the Apostle Paul to a pastor named Timothy. While the letter (epistle) is, of course, informative and enlightening for everyone, it is by context even more significant to pastors or Bible teachers. The ministry is commanded to preach and teach the Word of God:

**I charge thee therefore before God, and the Lord Jesus Christ, who shall judge the quick and the dead at his appearing and his kingdom; preach the word; be instant in season, out of season; reprove, rebuke, exhort with all longsuffering and doctrine (II Timothy 4:1-2).**

Now notice that they (pastors) are not commanded to teach just *anything*. They are instructed to continue teaching the same exact things that the apostles taught. This would serve as the only preventive remedy to counter the coming dilemma of Doctrinal Malnutrition.

**Take heed unto thyself, and unto the doctrine; continue in them: for in doing this thou shalt both save thyself, and them that hear thee (I Timothy 4:16).**

Now this kind of teaching can also be referred to as "feeding" the flock of God.

**Take heed therefore unto yourselves, and to all the flock, over the which the Holy Ghost hath made you overseers, to feed the church of God, which he hath purchased with his own blood. For I know this, that after my departing shall grevious wolves enter in among you, not sparing the flock (Acts 20:28-29).**

The ministry is commanded to "feed" and nourish the flock of God (church). A continual application and adherence to the apostles' doctrine is mandatory for a church's spiritual health and safety. Again, it is the only remedy to counter Doctrinal Malnutrition. Notice this event in the ministry of Jesus recorded in the Book of Mark:

**In those days the multitude being very great, and having nothing to eat, Jesus called his disciples unto him, and saith unto them, I have**

**compassion on the multitude, because they have now been with me three days, and have nothing to eat: And if I send them away fasting to their own houses, they will faint by the way: for divers of them come from far (Mark 8:1-3).**

If Jesus was moved with compassion to see a crowd of people who were physically hungry, how much more concerned is He today to see people who are *spiritually* hungry? People who are *doctrinally* malnourished and underfed?

In I Peter 2:2 the Apostle Peter tells us to "desire the sincere milk of the word." The Word of God is likened to a literal, healthy source of nourishment and strength. That word "sincere" means "pure," "genuine" or "unmixed." If one wishes to be spiritually strong, stable, mature and complete then one needs to feed upon the *pure* and first teachings of Jesus and His apostles. One doesn't need the mixtures, dilutions and alterations of other men that have gradually infiltrated Christianity through the years. I am firmly convinced that there are thousands of souls sitting on pews across America and throughout the entire world that are spiritually weak, spiritually undernourished and dying because of Doctrinal Malnutrition. Some precious and soul-saving promises that were once adamantly embraced and endorsed by the original founder(s) of Christianity have now been reduced to the status of secondary options and irrelevant rhetoric. I am also convinced that many good-hearted "Christians" are simply unaware of some of the primary and core commands of Christ and His apostles. It seems that Christianity today has gradually evolved into something that it was not at the beginning. It has in fact become infiltrated with so many different voices, ideas and philosophies that it is becoming ever more difficult for people to really know what to believe or which way to go. But I have some very good news. We do not have to be left in a state of confusion and despair. Fortunately we are left with a tool, a "compass" of sorts. We have been given a fool-proof method to help us distinguish between what is really true and what is not. And it's quite simple to use:

**We are of God: he that knoweth God heareth us; he that is not of God heareth not us. Hereby know we the spirit of truth, and the spirit of error (I John 4:6).**

This is how to discern between truth and error: If any person tells you to ignore any teaching or commandment of the apostles, they are not of God.

Period. It's that simple. Now I know that this passage of scripture (I John 4:6) isn't very popular or well-known by many. But personally I think it would be a very good idea for us to commit this scripture to memory and lodge it deep within our hearts in order for it to serve as a constant compass or guide to assist us in moments of questioning.

I remember hearing the story of a scuba diver who became disoriented far beneath the surface of the sea. He suddenly noticed that the bubbles from his breathing apparatus were heading downward instead of up. Now he knew in his mind and because of his training that the bubbles always go upwards to the surface of the water. Now he didn't *feel* disoriented at all. In his mind he believed that he needed to go in the opposite direction of the bubbles in order to reach the surface. But he knew that couldn't be right. So in spite of what he felt or what his mind perceived he began to follow the bubbles. The fear and sense of panic only increased as it seemed more and more that he was only going deeper in the wrong direction. But he forced himself to follow the bubbles in spite of his feelings. Suddenly he emerged safely at the surface of the water. Just as these bubbles led this man to natural safety, so will the words of Jesus and the apostles lead us to spiritual safety. Regardless of what we may feel like or what the majority of everyone else is believing and doing, we've got to make up our minds we're going to follow the words of Jesus and the apostles all the way through this sometimes disorienting event called "Life."

One of our greatest concerns should be to discover after it's too late that we've been spiritually deceived or misled. Even Jesus and the apostles warned us to do all we can to avoid spiritual deception:

**Beware of false prophets, which come to you in sheep's clothing, but inwardly they are ravening wolves (Matthew 7:15).**

**Beware lest any man spoil you through philosophy and vain deceit, after the tradition of men, after the rudiments of the world, and not after Christ (Colossians 2:8).**

**But there were false prophets also among the people, even as there shall be false teachers among you, who privily shall bring in damnable heresies, even denying the Lord that bought them, and bring upon themselves swift destruction (II Peter 2:1).**

**Beloved, believe not every spirit, but try the spirits whether they are of God: because many false prophets are gone out into the world (I John 4:1).**

Since spiritual deception is an awful and very real possibility it is ever so important that we consistently pray and endeavor to never become deceived or misled by any false way. There is nothing at all wrong with praying that way. We should regularly pray that we would always love truth, believe truth and obey truth. Now, call me crazy if you want to, but I have come to the conclusion that the safest and wisest thing to do is just stick with the original words and teachings of Jesus and the apostles no matter how unpopular they may *ever* become in society or among modern, twenty-first century Christianity. Let God be true but every man a liar (Romans 3:4).

Now let's get ready for an excavation. An unearthing of sorts. Not an excavation in search of mineral wealth, but an excavation of Divine Truths. You see, far beneath all of the layers of unscriptural clichés, man-made traditions, partial truths and blatant lies there is a vault. A vault of truth. And it is our privilege and responsibility to plummet the depths of

41

this man-made quagmire, seize the treasure and plunder the "jewels" contained within. And who knows? You may discover some "nuggets" of truth that you never even knew existed!

# Chapter Three

## Blinded By The Lie

There is a popular saying that is prevalent throughout Christianity today: "We are saved by grace alone." Many of the same people who espouse this conviction will also emphatically declare, "We are saved by faith alone." (Go figure). It is, of course, true that Christians are all saved by grace. Without the grace of God no one would be saved. But we must understand that Christians are not saved by grace *alone*. While grace is the primary root and common ingredient in everyone's salvation, it is not the *only* ingredient. (Now if your bottom jaw just dropped about three inches this is a good indication of Doctrinal Malnutrition. Keep reading). We must steer clear of any thought, inclination or philosophy that teaches that grace exempts us from any personal responsibility or obedience to certain and specific commands.

Now, for the record, let it first be known that I do believe in the devil. I believe in the existence of a literal being, an evil spirit that roams the earth wreaking havoc upon humanity and influencing people to do wrong. And his primary objective (contrary to what the televangelists may say) is not to wreak havoc upon your checkbook or your finances. His primary objective is not to afflict you with a physical disease or sickness, nor is it to depress you. His primary objective is to entice and lead the entire human race away from *obedience* to God's Word, the Bible. If you want to know what Satan is doing in the spiritual realm today, just look at what the serpent did in the natural realm thousands of years ago in the Book of Genesis:

**Now the serpent was more subtil than any beast of the field which the LORD God had made. And he said unto the woman, Yea, hath God said, Ye shall not eat of every tree of the garden? (Genesis 3:1).**

With the very first question appearing in the Bible we find the serpent encouraging disobedience to God's simple, plain and direct command. At the first mention of the serpent he is asking the question, "Hath God said?" In other words, "Did God *really* say what it sounded like He said?" "Does He *really* mean what it sounds like He means?" Well, today we still have to be watchful and cautious of that spirit of "Hath God Said?" It may come in a lot of different shapes, methods and styles but the underlying objective is consistent: Disobey God's Word! The primary objective of Satan is to entice people away from obedience to God's Word. And he will even use Scripture to accomplish this objective. That's precisely the reason why we must be aware of *all* that the Bible has to say about a particular subject. And when it comes to the subject of our salvation we'd better be thoroughly informed of what the Bible actually has to say.

God's grace does not exempt us from obedience to certain commands of God. In Genesis 6:8 we are told that "Noah found grace in the eyes of the LORD." God looked down upon a world that was filled with violence and gross immorality. In the midst of it all He took notice of a "preacher of righteousness" named Noah. He devised a plan to save Noah from this hostile environment while ridding the earth of its inhabitants as well. God told Noah to build an ark. He told him how big it should be and what kind of materials to use. He gave him very *detailed* and *specific* instructions. Just because Noah "found grace" did not mean that he was automatically saved whether he obeyed God or not. Noah *still* had a responsibility to obey God's command. Now, do you want to know what *also* saved Noah, according to the Word of God itself?

**By faith Noah, being warned of God...moved with fear, prepared an ark to the saving of his house... (Hebrews 11:7).**

The other thing that saved Noah (who found grace) was the fact that he "moved" and "prepared an ark" just as God instructed him to do. Because he *acted* on God's command and *obeyed* God's command, he and his family were saved. God's grace was absolutely necessary and essential in Noah's salvation. But God's grace did not exempt Noah from being obedient. He still had to build an ark if he wanted to be saved. Now I know at this point there may be some readers who have their mental wheels turning on how to dismantle this little analogy. But let me encourage you to keep reading. This is only a bullet compared to the arsenal ahead.

**For by grace are ye saved through faith; and that not of yourselves: it is the gift of God: not of works, lest any man should boast (Ephesians 2:8-9).**

When the Bible says that we are not saved by works it means that we are not saved by doing good deeds. Going to church, praying, donating money to charities and volunteering for community services are all well and fine but they do not earn us a reservation in heaven. But we are, however, saved by obedience to certain biblical commands. It's one thing to do good deeds but it's another thing entirely to obey certain scriptural commands.

First let's dismantle this misconception that we are saved by grace alone. Again, while grace is the root, essential and common ingredient in everyone's salvation—without the grace of God no one would be saved—it is not the only ingredient. Let's look at some other things that save us as well:

**But without faith it is impossible to please him: for he that cometh to God must believe that he is, and that he is a rewarder of them that diligently seek him (Hebrews 11:6).**

One essential ingredient in anyone's salvation is faith. In other words one must believe that He (God) exists and one must also believe that He (God) blesses and rewards those that diligently (actively, faithfully) seek Him.

**For we are saved by hope (Romans 8:24).**

Not only are Christians saved by grace and faith, but they are also saved by hope. The expectancy of what is yet to come (heaven and the deliverance from the afflictions and sufferings of this present world) often play a vital role in one's salvation. Hope helps to serve as an incentive or a motivation to keep faith and to endure hardships and trials. By the way, faith and hope are actually distinguished from each other as two separate and distinct things in I Corinthians 13.

**Not by works of righteousness which we have done, but according to his mercy he saved us, by the washing of regeneration, and renewing of the Holy Ghost (Titus 3:5).**

Not only are we saved by grace, faith and hope but we are also saved by God's mercy, the washing of regeneration and the renewing of the Holy Ghost. These latter two (the washing of regeneration and renewing of the Holy Ghost) will be defined and explored more deeply in later chapters.

**Moreover, brethren, I declare unto you the gospel which I preached unto you, which also ye**

**have received, and wherein ye stand; by which also ye are saved, if ye keep in memory what I preached unto you, unless ye have believed in vain (I Corinthians 15:1-2).**

Not only are we saved by grace, faith, hope, mercy, the washing of regeneration and the renewing of the Holy Ghost but did you know that we are also saved by the gospel? But notice there's a certain contingency that it's based upon. We have to keep in memory (keep believing and embracing) the things that Paul preached. There are a lot of people calling themselves "Christians" who do not keep in memory or high esteem the things that Paul preached. According to the Word of God they are believing in vain. Now this next one's a doozy. Brace yourself:

**Take heed unto thyself, and unto the doctrine; continue in them: for in doing this thou shalt both save thyself, and them that hear thee (I Timothy 4:16).**

Not only are we saved by grace, faith, hope, mercy, the washing of regeneration, the renewing of the Holy Ghost and the gospel (if we keep in memory the things that Paul preached) but we are also saved by continuing in the doctrine. And here is where much of

Christianity has dropped the ball. You see, a long, long time ago there were certain timeless, unchangeable teachings (doctrines) that were delivered by the Lord Jesus Christ and His apostles. These doctrines were unquestionably believed and embraced by Christianity for many years. It was in these same unchangeable doctrines that original Christianity was birthed and established. As long as Christianity remained in adherence to these same doctrines it was in its purest form. Yet somehow through time these same doctrines became neglected and dismissed as irrelevant. Little by little, throughout the centuries of church history, people slowly began to esteem the teachings of ordinary men *higher* than the teachings of Jesus Christ and the apostles.

What I mean by "ordinary" is the fact that the writings of these men were not divinely inspired by God Himself (as the Scriptures are) and their teachings are not infallible (as the apostles' are). These men were nowhere around when Jesus promised His disciples that they would be led into all truth (see John 16:13). Therefore it is a mistake to build one's doctrine upon their teachings instead of Scripture. Yet today many people are doing just that. Many don't even realize that they are embracing foreign ideas and impure teachings that are in fact directly opposing and contradicting the first, pure and *original* teachings of Jesus and the apostles. Remember, our doctrine should not differ from that of the apostles. And according to the apostle Paul, we are also saved by continuing in that *same* doctrine.

So we see then that we are saved by grace. We are saved by faith. We are saved by hope. We are saved by mercy. We are saved by the washing of regeneration. We are saved by the renewing of the Holy Ghost. We are saved by the gospel (if we keep in memory the things that Paul preached). And we are saved by continuing in the doctrine. By the way we are also saved by continuing in God's goodness (Romans 11:22), receiving the engrafted Word of God with meekness (James 1:21), and by the foolishness of preaching (I Corinthians 1:21). Again, while grace is the common ingredient in everyone's salvation, and without the grace of God no one would be saved, it is not the only ingredient. Consider this for an example: Is there any one individual that is kept alive by his brain alone? After all, without the brain every vital organ would instantly shut down. Right? So surely we must be kept alive by the brain alone! But what if the brain remained healthy and intact but the heart suddenly shut down? Ah, so it must be the heart then that keeps us alive! But what if the lungs suddenly failed? How long would an individual live without his lungs? What about the liver? What about the kidneys? Just as the body sustains life by all these organs working together, so too is salvation the result of several factors combined.

Now prepare to be enlightened by the Lord Jesus Christ and His apostles as to just how important a little thing called "obedience" actually is. Because according to these men, we are also saved by obedience.

**Not every one that saith unto me, Lord, Lord, shall enter into the kingdom of heaven; but he that doeth the will of my Father which is in heaven. Many will say unto me in that day, Lord, Lord, have we not prophesied in thy name? and in thy name have cast out devils? and in thy name done many wonderful works? And then will I profess unto them, I never knew you: depart from me, ye that work iniquity (Matthew 7:21-23).**

This should be a very sobering passage for anyone who claims to be a Christian. It's not enough to just recognize the deity or lordship of Jesus Christ. There has to be some obedience. Recognizing Him or "accepting" Him as Lord is only the beginning. That's the foundation. That is where it all starts. Some time ago my four-year-old son, in exasperation, asked my wife if he could please quit school once he finished learning his numbers and the letters of the alphabet. That is exactly the same mentality of a lot of Christians. They confess or acknowledge Him as "Lord" and then go back to life as usual. People who have the brazen audacity to ignore overtly plain and obvious commands of scripture while still claiming to be "believers" are grossly deceived. Even Jesus had to ask this question:

**And why call ye me, Lord, Lord, and do not the things which I say? Whosoever cometh to me, and heareth my sayings, and doeth them, I will shew you to whom he is like: He is like a man which built an house, and digged deep, and laid the foundation on a rock: and when the flood arose, the stream beat vehemently upon that house, and could not shake it: for it was founded upon a rock. But he that heareth, and doeth not, is like a man that without a foundation built a house upon the earth; against which the stream did beat vehemently, and immediately it fell; and the ruin of that house was great (Luke 6:46-49).**

This scripture should change your entire outlook upon every single word of Jesus and the apostles. You may have heard this passage of scripture ever since your childhood. But hearing it and believing it are two separate things. Obedience matters. Still not convinced? Look at what the Apostle Paul told the Christians at Rome:

**But God be thanked, that ye were the servants of sin, but ye have obeyed from the heart that form of doctrine which was delivered you (Romans 6:17).**

He thanked God that they *were* (past tense) the servants of sin. But what happened to save them from that dire condition? There was a certain doctrine that was delivered unto them and they what? They obeyed it.

**And being made perfect, he became the author of eternal salvation unto all them that obey him (Hebrews 5:9).**

Let it be understood that without the shed blood of Christ this entire discourse would be pointless. But because Jesus died on the cross doesn't mean that the whole world automatically became saved. Jesus died on the cross so that humanity could have access to God. We were all once afar off but now we are made nigh (near) by the blood of Christ (Ephesians 2:13). Jesus is not the author of eternal salvation for anyone and everyone that ever lived. He is the author of eternal salvation unto all them that obey Him.

**Ye have purified your souls in obeying the truth (I Peter 1:22).**

Would you like your soul purified? Obey the truth.

**What shall the end be of them that obey not the gospel of God? (I Peter 4:17).**

Paul answered that question:

**The Lord Jesus shall be revealed from heaven with his mighty angels, in flaming fire taking vengeance on them that know not God, and that obey not the gospel of our Lord Jesus Christ (II Thessalonians 1:7).**

So we see then that obedience does play a vital role in one's salvation. Don't let anyone mislead you into believing that it doesn't.

Now there are some specific commandments that are directly related to salvation. Obedience to these commands engages us *fully* into New Covenant Christianity. Now let's just take a look at those commands. First we'll only briefly observe their references; then in the following chapters we'll define and explore each one separately and in detail.

**Except ye repent, ye shall all likewise perish (Luke 13:3).**

**God...commandeth all men everywhere to repent (Acts 17:30).**

**The Lord is...not willing that any should perish, but that all should come to repentance (II Peter 3:9).**

It does not matter how eloquent, smart or famous he or she may be, do not allow a preacher, teacher, writer or anyone (directly or indirectly) to lead you into believing that repentance doesn't matter.

He that believeth and is baptized shall be saved; but he that believeth not shall be damned (Mark 16:16).

And now why tarriest thou? Arise, and be baptized, and wash away thy sins, calling on the name of the Lord (Acts 22:16).

Know ye not, that so many of us as were baptized into Jesus Christ were baptized into his death? Therefore we are buried with him by baptism into death: that like as Christ was raised up from the dead by the glory of the Father, even so we also should walk in newness of life. For if we have been planted together in the likeness of his death, we shall also be in the likeness of his resurrection (Romans 6:3-5).

For as many of you as have been baptized into Christ have put on Christ (Galatians 3:27).

The like figure whereunto even baptism doth also now save us (not the putting away of the filth of the flesh, but the answer of a good conscience toward God,) by the resurrection of Jesus Christ (I Peter 3:21).

Remember, each of these passages of scripture will be thoroughly explored in a subsequent chapter.

**He that believeth on me, as the scripture hath said, out of his belly shall flow rivers of living water. (But this spake he of the Spirit, which they that believe on him should receive: for the Holy Ghost was not yet given; should receive: for the Holy Ghost was not yet given; 39).**

**So then they that are in the flesh cannot please God. But ye are not in the flesh, but in the Spirit, if so be that the Spirit of God dwell in you. Now if any man have not the Spirit of Christ, he is none of his (Romans 8:8-9).**

**And be not drunk with wine, wherein is excess; but be filled with the Spirit (Ephesians 5:18).**

Please understand that this infilling (receiving or baptism) of the Holy Ghost is not a special privilege reserved for only a select few individuals. As we will see ahead, it is in fact an extremely vital experience that lies at the very core of the New Covenant (New Testament).

Remember, when it comes to the subject of our salvation we need to be sure that we are right in line and in direct accordance with the teachings of the Lord Jesus Christ and His disciples.

# Chapter Four

## The Fruit of Godly Sorrow

Within the Bible we find many different men and women that were powerfully utilized by God in order to bring about change and moral progress amongst His people. There were certain individuals that were raised up and uniquely commissioned by God Himself to step onto the scene at crucial moments in the nation of Israel's history. On God's behalf they would preach and prophesy and boldly declare what the will of God was. These prophets and leaders were mightily empowered by the Spirit of God. And of course it is only proper that we hold them in high esteem. But there was a certain man of God that Jesus Himself referred to as "a prophet and more than a prophet." He was John the Baptist.

**In those days came John the Baptist, preaching in the wilderness of Judaea, and saying, Repent ye: for the kingdom of heaven is at hand...And the same John had his raiment of camel's hair, and a leathern girdle about his loins;**

**and his meat was locusts and wild honey. Then
went out to him Jerusalem, and all Judaea, and all
the region round about Jordan, and were baptized
of him in Jordan, confessing their sins (Matthew
3:1-3;5-6).**

John the Baptist was born of a priestly
heritage. His father was a Judaic priest by the name of
Zacharias. His mother was a direct physical
descendant of Aaron himself (the very first high
priest). The Bible tells us that John grew and became
strong in spirit. That means he wasn't timid, reluctant
or a bit slow to speak the truth. He lived and preached
in the wilderness and clothed himself in camel's hair.
His diet consisted of locusts and honey. Now no doubt
there were some who considered him to be some type
of a "fanatic" or a "radical." (God's prophets usually
were considered such). They always possessed those
certain, unique qualities and characteristics that the
times demanded in order to bring about a significant
change. These were the kinds of individuals that *really*
made a difference. Now we can use our imaginations
and suppose that John the Baptist was quite often the
subject of many heated conversations: "Why I heard
him call those poor fellows a bunch of vipers! Right
while he was preaching!" "Can you imagine that man?
Living in the wilderness like an animal, preaching like

a wild man?" "Hey, Zacharias, maybe you should have a little talk with your son.

But Zacharias could often think back and remember that day in the temple when an angel appeared to him. The angel told him that Elisabeth was going to have a son and they were to name him "John." He was told that John would be great in the sight of the Lord and that he would be filled with the Holy Ghost from his mother's womb. He would turn the hearts of many in Israel back to God and he would turn the disobedient to the wisdom of the just. He would make ready a people prepared for the Lord! Maybe Zacharias didn't understand it entirely, but one thing he knew for sure was that his son was obviously preparing the way for something big. You see, in the divine plan of God there had to be a John the Baptist before there would be a ministry of Jesus Christ. John the Baptist was hand-picked and commissioned by God to create a certain climate (environment) in Israel that would be conducive for them to receive their Messiah. God raised up a prophet that would make ready a people *prepared* for the Lord. Whenever it came time for a deep, genuine conversion and a significant change amongst God's people, God never sent a coddler. He sent men with fervor and passion. He sent men who were unafraid to declare the will of

God. Now the very first spoken words that we find recorded of John in the New Testament actually embodied his entire ministry and purpose:

**In those days came John the Baptist, preaching in the wilderness of Judaea, and saying, Repent ye: for the kingdom of heaven is at hand (Matthew 3:1-2).**

It mattered not to John if you were a barbaric Roman solider, a "religious" official or even a king. The message was the same: Repent! And thus began one of the most fundamental and primary doctrines of the New Testament concerning salvation. Well, today things are no different from what they were in John's day. That which was required of everyone then is still required of everyone now: Repent! Even the Lord Jesus Christ Himself said:

**Except ye repent, ye shall all likewise perish (Luke 13:3).**

You will notice that this was not some lone isolated comment directed only to the hearers of Jesus' words that day, but it is in fact a command directed to every human being in every place everywhere. Paul had this to say:

**God...commandeth all men everywhere to repent (Acts 17:30).**

Peter had this to say:

**The Lord is...not willing that any should perish, but that all should come to repentance (II Peter 3:9).**

It is interesting to me how often this vital ingredient seems to be left out and not even mentioned by our modern "Christian" artists, entertainers and traveling evangelistic faith-healers when it comes to the subject of salvation. If an individual truly believes "in" or "on" Jesus it means that he will obey Jesus. It is absurd to claim a belief in Jesus and then ignore Him. Once an individual "believes" in Jesus the first thing he needs to do is repent. Now there are many varied definitions out there of what repentance is but why don't we look to Jesus and the Bible itself for the clearest definition and understanding of the word. In Matthew 12:41 and Luke 11:32 Jesus said that the men of Nineveh repented at the preaching of Jonah. Now if Jesus said that they repented, then it's safe to assume that they did. Therefore it behooves us to see *what* they did in order for us to get a clear understanding of the word.

**And God saw their works, that they turned from their evil way (Jonah 3:10).**

God noticed an active response to Jonah's preaching. And He noticed a visible, distinguishable change in their behavior. The New Testament word for "repentance" is "metanoeo" and it literally means "to change." It reflects a change in thinking which then produces a change in behavior. Repentance initially involves asking God to forgive us of anything and everything we've done wrong in our lives. And then, from that point on, we endeavor to live a life in accordance with and obedience to His Word. That is true repentance. Repentance doesn't mean that you've now become perfect, but remember, it does mean you've made a change. A change that affects you mentally, spiritually and yes even physically. When you truly recognize and acknowledge the fact that Jesus Christ is **LORD**, a major paradigm shift should occur in your life. He is now the Master; you are the slave. He is now the Teacher; you are the student. Notice what Paul said about repentance:

**Now I rejoice, not that ye were made sorry, but that ye sorrowed to repentance: for ye were made sorry after a godly manner...for godly sorrow worketh repentance to salvation...for**

**behold this selfsame thing, that ye sorrowed after a godly sort, what carefulness it wrought in you, yea, what clearing of yourselves, yea, what indignation, yea, what fear, yea, what vehement desire, yea, what revenge! In all things you have approved yourselves to be clear in this manner (II Corinthians 7:9-11).**

The Apostle Paul stated here that "godly sorrow" produces a genuine repentance. A repentance that then fosters indignation, a passion for righteousness, spiritual zeal and even a fear of God. Godly sorrow produces a repentance that manifests and reflects a notable change in one's life—a change for good. So what then is "godly sorrow"? Godly sorrow can be defined as a "good guilt." A healthy acknowledgment or recognition of the fact that one is indeed guilty and the ability to "feel" bad about doing bad. Now let's discuss godly sorrow. Paul said:

**There is therefore now no condemnation to them which are in Christ Jesus, who walk not after the flesh, but after the Spirit (Romans 8:1).**

I have noticed some that have casually utilized this passage as some sort of a "safety net" or a "shield" to protect them from feeling any condemnation or guilt, even if they are in fact guilty! Even if they've mistreated someone or lied you still may get, "Oh well, there is therefore now no condemnation...." The passage says that there is no condemnation to them in Christ Jesus who walk after the Spirit. Apparently, there is however, condemnation remaining to them which walk after the flesh.

So what then does it mean to walk after the flesh? To walk after the flesh means you choose to serve your own will above God's will. Your desires and personal preferences matter more than God's. And if we voluntarily choose to consistently walk after the flesh, ultimately there is condemnation:

**Now the works of the flesh are manifest, which are these; adultery, fornication, uncleanness, lasciviousness, idolatry, witchcraft, hatred, variance, emulations, wrath, strife, seditions, heresies, envyings, murders, drunkenness, revellings, and such like: of the which I tell you before, as I have also told you in time past, that they which do such things shall not inherit the kingdom of God (Galatians 5:19-21).**

As mentioned earlier it seems that some use Romans 8:1 as a scapegoat clause to mean: "Even if I do wrong it's still okay because there is no condemnation to them who are in Christ Jesus." Perhaps it is just an automatic response or some type of "defense mechanism" that kicks in at an attempt to alleviate any "feelings" of remorse for something done wrong. Instead of just facing up to the fault they try to ignore it. But I contend that sometimes a little bit of guilt (godly sorrow) can be a good thing. If I've done something wrong, I want to know it. I don't want to continue on in blind ignorance, unaware of my follies and transgressions. If we are doing something wrong or displeasing to God we need to be made aware of it. There needs to be a sense of uneasiness or conviction about it. Something's terribly wrong if there's not.

**And herein do I exercise myself, to have always a conscience void of offence toward God, and toward men (Acts 24:16).**

Godly sorrow, then, is a God-given consciousness and an awareness that can compel us to make things right. In fact, godly sorrow can make us miserable until we *do* make things right. Having this God-given ability is one of the things that separate us from the animal kingdom. You see, we all possess a certain amount of dignity about us just because we're human. In fact, there is even a certain element of

69

"divinity" within *every* human being simply because he is human. We as human beings are eternally living spirits housed within temporary, fleshly bodies. Bodies that were made in the image of God Himself! And we were not put on this earth to think, act, behave and live like common animals. We have a much higher calling than that. We are here to serve our Creator with a certain dignity that is reminiscent of His own dignity. We are here to serve God in obedience and holiness according to *His* rules. We should consider ourselves very fortunate that we possess this awareness and ability to know who He is and what He expects and desires from us. We should be thankful that we even have a conscience that is capable of feeling remorse. Just feeling remorse, however, is not enough to save us. It is only the inner monitor that guides us in the right direction. Here is an example of godly sorrow in action:

**Therefore let all the house of Israel know assuredly that God hath made that same Jesus, whom ye have crucified, both Lord and Christ. Now when they heard this they were pricked in their heart, and said unto Peter and to the rest of the apostles, Men and brethren, what shall we do? Then Peter said unto them, Repent... (Acts 2:36-38).**

When Peter declared to the crowd that Jesus was both Lord and Christ (God and the Messiah) and that they had brutally crucified Him, something happened deep inside of them. They were "pricked in their hearts." Something broke on the inside and they were now standing in the prime condition and perfect frame of mind to finally cry out, "What shall we do?" Their hearts were laid open to receive the remedy for their sin-stricken souls. We are again living in days when we need this same kind of heart–cutting preaching. Preaching that declares plainly what is right and what is wrong according to the Word of God. Preaching that fosters a godly sorrow, breaks hearts and humbles proud spirits. Why? Because:

**The LORD is nigh unto them that are of a broken heart; and saveth such as be of a contrite spirit (Psalm 34:18).**

**Thus saith the LORD, The heaven is my throne, and the earth is my footstool...but to this man will I look, even to him that is poor and of a contrite spirit, and trembleth at my word (Isaiah 66:1-2).**

Even though He is the Almighty Creator of the heavens and the earth, He is never too high to heed the prayer of a humble, broken man.

It is said that much of what we are or ever become depends greatly upon our decisions. I've heard it said, "We make our decisions, and then our decisions make us." The truth is, even the destiny of our souls can depend much upon how we respond to our guilt. Peter and Judas both betrayed and denied Christ. But each one reacted differently to his guilt. One became a powerful, influential apostle who wrote part of the New Testament. The other committed suicide. Guilt that is not properly dealt with can render an individual spiritually "paralyzed," feeling immersed and powerlessly lost within a sphere of hopelessness. If there is an unhealthy pondering and preoccupation with all of our own faults, weaknesses, temptations, inconsistencies and failures it will rob us of ever becoming effective, influential Christians. This is where a good understanding of the power of the blood of Jesus comes in:

**But if we walk in the light, as he is in the light, we have fellowship one with another, and the blood of Jesus Christ, his Son, cleanseth us from all sin (I John 1:7).**

Walking in the light does not mean walking in perfection and never falling. It means walking in the knowledge of who Jesus really is (God in flesh) and believing His words to be true. This "light" enables us to see (recognize and identify) what is sin. Once we recognize sin, we are privileged to have access today to the same blood of Jesus that was shed at the Crucifixion to cleanse us from our sin. The next verse tells us how to access and apply the blood:

**If we say that we have no sin, we deceive ourselves, and the truth is not in us. If we confess our sins, he is faithful and just to forgive us our sins, and to cleanse us from all unrighteousness (I John 1:8-9).**

That word "faithful" means "every time." The cleansing power of the blood of Jesus is a consistently reliable source of soul-cleansing in time of need.

Of course, God is very displeased with our sins and our wrongdoings. Not only do we suffer for them but quite often others suffer as well. The truth is some people may never forgive us for the things we've done. The embarrassment, shame, heartache or misery that we may have caused others may never be forgotten by some people. But we do have to realize that God does fervently love us. We were born on this earth to be His own children. And in spite of our past sins, our present sins and even our future sins, there must come a time when we finally cross that line and enter into that dimension where Jesus Christ truly, really, genuinely is LORD.

**Let us therefore come boldly unto the throne of grace, that we may obtain mercy, and find grace to help in time of need (Hebrews 4:16).**

# Chapter Five

## The Significance of Baptism

In this chapter we are going to discover and thoroughly explore the profound and divine significance of water baptism. This highly important practice has undergone some very interesting changes through time. Much of what is *called* baptism today is in reality a strange variation from what it was originally in the beginning. Remember, the New Testament is our role model and pattern, not the recent traditions and modern alternative practices of men.

One interesting variation that has evolved through time is the idea that baptism is merely a ceremonious ritual that has no salvific (saving) value to it at all. But that is exactly the opposite of what Jesus and the apostles taught. There is much evidence to support the idea that water baptism is in fact directly connected to salvation. First of all let's consider the saving aspect of baptism. The Lord Jesus Christ said these words:

**He that believeth and is baptized shall be saved; but he that believeth not shall be damned (Mark 16:16).**

Now I know that there are many "enlightened" men today who seem to know a little more about this than Jesus. Perhaps they believe we should be thankful that they finally arrived to set things right. Why there are even some who have put such a twist on this passage as to have us actually believe, in the final analysis that what Jesus *really* meant here was, "He that believeth and is *not* baptized shall still be saved anyway." But there's only one tiny, little problem with that. That's not what it says. Let's just use our imaginations and continue in this same strange logic. For example, let's just say you made an agreement with an individual and even went so far as to put *in writing* a statement that said, "If you mow my front yard *and* wash my car, I'll give you 100 dollars." And let's just say this individual only mowed your front lawn. Will you gladly pay him the 100 dollars? No. Why is it then that when God Himself makes an agreement, a covenantal stipulation, and even puts it *in writing*, people are so quick and insolent as to say, "Well, that's not what it *really* means!" Just try this same logic with the policeman. "Yes, officer, I know the sign says 'Stop', but I know that it really means

'Do *not* stop'." Or try it with your employer, "Yes sir, I know the contract states that I am to wear a hard hat and steel-toe boots on the job site, but my buddy told me that I really *don't* have to wear the hard hat. And he went to college!" I know it may seem, on the surface, a needless point to state, but honestly, sometimes we need to reassess and reevaluate the authority of our sources when formulating doctrinal decisions. We need to ask ourselves who we are ultimately going to believe. Jesus or Charles Swindoll? The apostles or Pastor "Bob"? Again, there is an abundantly overwhelming amount of biblical evidence to support the idea that baptism is in fact directly connected to salvation. Here's what the Apostle Peter said:

**Then Peter said unto them, Repent, and be baptized every one of you in the name of Jesus Christ for the remission of sins (Acts 2:38).**

That word translated "remission" comes from the Greek word "aphesin" and it literally means "forgiveness." There are some who have used this passage to endorse the idea that, according to Acts 2:38, baptism should be administered because we've already been forgiven. Let's just quickly reconsider the verse in that context to see how absurd that reasoning would be. According to our modern "experts" the passage (Acts 2:36-38) *should* read something like this: "Therefore let all the house of Israel know assuredly, that God hath made that same Jesus, whom ye have crucified, both Lord and Christ. Now when they heard this, they were pricked in their heart, and said unto Peter and the rest of the apostles, Men and brethren, what shall we do? Then Peter said unto them, Repent, and be baptized every one of you in the name of Jesus Christ because you've already been forgiven." It is also very interesting to point out that another place in the New Testament that you find these words "for the remission of sins" is when Jesus said "This is my blood...which is shed for many for the remission of sins" (Matthew 26:28). No one would say that Jesus shed His blood because we have already been forgiven. Neither should we suggest that baptism is to be administered because forgiveness is already obtained. Even the original Greek grammatical structure in Acts 2:38 is identical to that in Matthew 26:28, "eis aphesin hamartian" (for the remission of sins). I know it may cross some modern theology, but Peter plainly stated that baptism is for the remission of sins. Remember, as observed in chapter 3, there are several components combined in salvation. And according to the Bible, baptism is one of those components.

**And now why tarriest thou? arise, and be baptized, and wash away thy sins, calling on the name of the Lord (Acts 22:16).**

Now I realize that it may be only a coincidence that the words "be baptized" and "wash away thy sins" appear side by side, in the same sentence, in the same verse, but I rather doubt it.

**Know ye not, that so many of us as were baptized into Jesus Christ were baptized into his death? Therefore we are buried with him by baptism into death: that like as Christ was raised up from the dead by the glory of the Father, even so we also should walk in newness of life. For if we have been planted together in the likeness of his death, we shall be also in the likeness of his resurrection (Romans 6:3-5).**

**For as many of you as have been baptized into Christ have put on Christ (Galatians 3:27).**

When we repent and have an all-out faith in Christ (believing that He is who He says He is) and we *sincerely* acknowledge His Lordship and deity, a certain "death" should occur in our lives—a death to self. The pattern to follow this "death" is a "burial."

Paul said here that we are buried with Him by baptism. And *if* we have been planted together with Him in this type of burial, we will also be in the likeness of His resurrection.

**Not by works of righteousness which we have done, but according to his mercy he saved us, by the washing of regeneration, and renewing of the Holy Ghost (Titus 3:5).**

In light of all of the passages that directly connect baptism to salvation, it becomes highly likely that this "washing of regeneration" refers to water baptism. Baptism is not a work of righteousness (good deed). It is the response of a truly converted conscience. Notice this next verse:

**Which sometime were disobedient when once the longsuffering of God waited in the days of Noah, while the ark was a preparing, wherein few, that is eight souls were saved by water. The like figure whereunto even baptism doth also now save us (not the putting away of the filth of the flesh, but the answer of a good conscience toward God,) by the resurrection of Jesus Christ (I Peter 3:20-21).**

At first it may seem strange to suggest that Noah and his family were "saved by water." After all, wasn't it the *water* that they were escaping? Was it not the *ark* that actually saved them? But Peter specifically states that Noah and his family were saved by the water. Is this perhaps a biblical typo? No, this is just an example of a passage that needs to be explored deeply. You see, one of the main purposes for the writing of I Peter was to strengthen and encourage the church in the midst of sufferings and persecutions. A central theme of this epistle is the certainty of God's ability to preserve his people in the midst of hostile persecutions (see I Peter 3:12-14). It is precisely in this context that Peter stated that Noah and his family were "saved by water." Noah was a preacher of righteousness (I Peter 2:5) in the midst of a world filled with violence (Genesis 6:11). Just as God used the Nile River (water) to save Moses from the sword of Pharaoh, and God used the Red Sea (water) to save the Israelites from an impending massacre by the Egyptian military, so too did God use the flood (water) to save Noah from a wicked world filled with violence. Of course it was *God* that saved the baby Moses, but water was utilized in His plan. Of course it was *God* that saved the Israelites, but again, water was utilized in His plan. And of course *God* saved Noah, but again, water was a means utilized. And according to the Apostle Peter this is a like figure of the fact that baptism does also save us. God is once again using water in a plan of salvation. Peter is quick to mention that it is not the physical act itself that saves, but the fact that it is the answer (response) of a good (convinced, converted) conscience. In order for a baptism to be effective it must be combined with an absolute faith in Jesus Christ. Otherwise one just got wet! This is one reason why the baptizing of infants is ultimately unprofitable. A baptism needs to be the self-made decision of an individual whose conscience is convicted, convinced and converted to the person of Jesus Christ. Furthermore, we have no record or instruction of infant baptism anywhere in Scripture.

Seeing then that baptism plays such a vital role in authentic, original Christianity it is ever so important that we look to the Bible itself to see just exactly how it is to be administered and practiced. First of all, the word "baptize" comes from the Greek word "baptidzo," and it literally means to "immerse" or "submerge." If Jesus and the apostles intended for this act to transpire through the means of sprinkling it would be called by another name entirely. The Greek word for "sprinkling" is "rhaintidzo." We would all be instructed to be "rhaintized" instead of "baptized." Also, if Jesus and the apostles intended for baptism to be done by the means of sprinkling we would see it practiced and endorsed in the Bible, but we don't. Remember, the Bible is our role model and blueprint, not the modern traditions and practices of men. Remember what Paul said:

**Know ye not, that so many of us as were baptized into Jesus Christ were baptized into his death? Therefore we are buried with him by baptism into death…for if we have been planted together in the likeness of his death, we shall also be in the likeness of his resurrection (Romans 6:3-5).**

Baptism is a type of "burial." When we bury someone we cover them. We don't sprinkle dirt on them. Remember, the word literally means to immerse or submerge. Notice this:

**And Jesus, when he was baptized, went up straightway out of the water: and lo, the heavens were opened unto him, and he saw the Spirit of God descending like a dove, and lighting upon him (Matthew 3:16).**

Before Jesus could come up straightway out of the water, He had to first go down into the water. Notice this also:

**And as they went on their way, they came unto a certain water: and the eunuch said, see, here is water; what doth hinder me to be baptized? And Philip said, if thou believest with all thine heart, thou mayest. And he answered and said, I believe that Jesus Christ is the son of God. And he commanded the chariot to stand still: and they went down both into the water, both Philip and the eunuch; and he baptized him. And when they were come up out of the water, the Spirit of the Lord caught away Philip, that the eunuch saw him no more: and he went on his way rejoicing (Acts 8:36-39).**

Notice that Philip led the eunuch directly into the water and there he baptized (submerged, immersed)                                          him.
Secondly, we notice in the Bible that baptism is always to be done in the name of Jesus Christ.

**Then Peter said unto them, Repent, and be baptized every one of you in the name of Jesus Christ for the remission of sins (Acts 2:38).**

**Now when the apostles which were at Jerusalem heard that Samaria had received the word of God, they sent unto them Peter and John: who, when they were come down, prayed for them, that they might receive the Holy Ghost: (for as yet he was fallen upon none of them: only they were baptized in the name of the Lord Jesus) (Acts 8:14-16).**

The Apostle Peter again:

**Can any man forbid water, that these should not be baptized, which have received the Holy Ghost as well as we? And he commanded them to be baptized in the name of the Lord (Acts 10:47-48).**

The Apostle Paul also endorsed baptism in Jesus' name:

**Then said Paul, John verily baptized with the baptism of repentance, saying unto the people, that they should believe on him which should come after him, that is, on Christ Jesus. When they heard this, they were baptized in the name of the Lord Jesus (Acts 19:4-5).**

The Book of Acts is perhaps one of the most important and foundational books in the entire Bible. It is here that we observe the birth and formation of Christianity. In the Book of Acts we find just exactly what the apostles taught and commanded in order to become a Christian. It was in their teachings that true Christianity was birthed, formed, nurtured and established. This was the church in its purest form. Nothing should have changed since. Our doctrine should not differ from that of the apostles.

Seeing then that baptism is to be done in the name of Jesus, it behooves us to search the Scriptures in order to discover exactly what that means and how to actually do it. In Mark 16 Jesus said that His disciples would cast out devils in His name. In Acts 16 we see this promise fulfilled. Notice how the Apostle Paul dispelled an evil spirit in the name of Jesus:

**And this did she many days. But Paul, being grieved, turned and said to the spirit, I command thee in the name of Jesus Christ to come out of her. And he came out the same hour (Acts 16:18).**

The Apostle Paul cast out this spirit in the name of Jesus by literally invoking (with faith) the words "in the name of Jesus Christ." Again, in Mark

16 Jesus instructed His disciples that they would heal in the name of Jesus. In Acts 3 we see this accomplished. Notice how Peter healed a lame man in the name of Jesus:

**Then Peter said, Silver and gold have I none; but such as I have give I thee: In the name of Jesus Christ of Nazareth rise up and walk (Acts 3:6).**

The Apostle Peter invoked the power and presence of God to heal when he (with faith) spoke the words "in the name of Jesus Christ." Therefore it is reasonable to conclude that in order for a baptism to be properly administered in Jesus' name, these same words should be audibly invoked by us as well at the point of administering a baptism.

**And now why tarriest thou? arise, and be baptized, and wash away thy sins, calling on the name of the Lord (Acts 22:16).**

Now this next passage of scripture is highly enlightening:

**And Jesus came and spake unto them, saying, All power is given unto me in heaven and in**

**earth. Go ye therefore, and teach all nations, baptizing them in the name of the Father, and of the Son, and of the Holy Ghost (Matthew 28:18-19).**

What just happened here? We just observed that the apostles always and only baptized in the name of Jesus, yet we find here they were instructed to baptize in the name of the Father, and of the Son, and of the Holy Ghost. Did the apostles erroneously or blatantly disobey Jesus when they baptized in His name? Or did they accurately fulfill this command when they baptized in His name? It's got to be one or the other. Personally, I believe they accurately fulfilled His command. Here's why: Jesus just claimed here to be the sole possessor of all the power in heaven and earth. He said all the power belongs to "Me." Then He said, "Therefore" (because of that) go and baptize in the "Name" (singular) of the Father, Son and Holy Ghost. This was a more formal way for Him to plainly declare and reveal the fact that all of the Godhead (nature or essence of God) dwells completely within Himself.

According to Colossians 2:9-10 the "fullness" of the Godhead dwells within Jesus Christ bodily. That word "fullness" comes from the Greek word "pleroma" and it literally means "totality." All that ever was God or is God or ever will be God resides and dwells totally, fully and completely in Jesus Christ. He is the head of all principality and power. And we are complete in Him (singular pronoun). We're not incomplete, partially correct or leaving anyone out if our faith is in Him. The terminology utilized in Matthew 28:19 was just a much more formal or elaborate way for Him to command baptism to be administered in His name. It was not uncommon for Jesus to occasionally refer to Himself in formal or elaborate titles and terminology. (The Good Shepherd, The Door, The Way, The Truth, The Life, The Resurrection, The First and The Last, The Alpha and Omega, The King, Bread of Heaven, etc.) What if He said to baptize in the name of the Good Shepherd? But what is the name of the Good Shepherd? Jesus. What if He said to baptize in the name of The Door? What is the name of the Door? Jesus. Father, Son and Holy Ghost is not the final name of the one true God. The Final name of the one true God is Jesus. His disciples clearly and correctly understood this profound and penetrating revelation in Matthew 28:19 and so they correctly, obediently and accurately fulfilled His command when they went and baptized "in the name of Jesus." Not only was this the normal and common mode of baptism in original Christianity throughout the entire New Testament, but it was also the common mode for the first several years of church history. Now just in case the Bible fails to serve as an adequate source of reliability for some readers, perhaps the following information will prove to be more helpful:

*"The formula used was 'in the name of Jesus Christ'...there is no evidence for the use of the trine name."* —Encyclopedia of Religion and Ethics, Vol. 2, p. 384.

*"...baptism in early Christianity was administered not in the threefold name but 'in the name of Jesus Christ' or 'in the name of the Lord Jesus'."* —Interpreter's Dictionary of the Bible, Vol. 1, p. 351.

*"At first baptism was administered in the name of Jesus..."* —Otto Heick, A History of Christian thought, Vol. 1, p. 53.

*"...The original form of words was 'into the name of Jesus Christ' or 'The Lord Jesus.' Baptism into the name of the Trinity was a later development."* —Hasting's Dictionary of the Bible, Vol. 1, p. 241.

*"The Trinitarian baptismal formula...was displacing the older baptism in the name of Christ."*

—Williston Walker, A History of the Christian Church, p. 58.

*"The New Testament knows only baptism in the name of Jesus... which still occurs even in the second and third centuries."* —The New Schaff-Herzog Encyclopedia of Religious Knowledge, Vol. 1, p. 435.

*"Persons were baptized at first 'in the name of Jesus Christ'...or ' in the name of the Lord Jesus'. ...Afterwards, with the development of the doctrine of the Trinity, they were baptized ' in the name of the Father and of the Son and of the Holy Ghost.'"* — Canney's Encyclopedia of Religions, p. 53

*"It is natural to conclude that baptism was administered in the earliest times 'in the name of Jesus Christ' or in that 'of the Lord Jesus.' This view is confirmed by the fact that the earliest forms of the baptismal confession appear to have been single—not triple, as was the later creed"* —Encyclopedia Biblica, Vol.1, p. 473.

*"The Trinitarian formula and trine immersion were not uniformly used from the beginning...Bapti[sm] into the name of the Lord [was]*

*the normal formula of the New Testament. In the 3rd century baptism in the name of Christ was still so widespread that Pope Stephen...declared it to be valid."* —Encyclopedia Britannica, 11th edition, Vol. 2, p. 365. [1]

Since our doctrine should not differ from that of the apostles, baptism today should be administered for the remission of sins, by full immersion into water and in the name of Jesus Christ, just as Jesus and His apostles commanded and endorsed.

# Chapter Six

## A Divine Encounter With Fire

Without a doubt, the absolute most magnanimous event that a human being can ever experience is the baptism (infilling or receiving) of the Holy Ghost (Spirit of God). Now I know that within our lives we experience many monumental moments or landmark events (the birth of a child, a marriage or a graduation). But in spite of all those awesome occurrences I firmly believe that the greatest thing that can ever happen to a person is the receiving of the Holy Ghost. Now it is very important that we don't mentally dismiss this experience as something that was only available or possible many, many years ago. Nor should we consider it to be merely an "extra blessing" for a select few Christians here and there that God randomly chooses. The Bible plainly declares that it is the will of God for every individual who considers himself to be a Christian to be filled with the Holy Ghost.

Contained within the pages of the Old Testament there is found what is commonly referred to as "the law". Sometimes it is referred to as "the law of Moses" or "the Mosaic law". The law was given by God to the nation of Israel and it consisted of over six hundred commandments that governed them in such matters as diet, how to farm their land, how to dress, etc. The law also governed them in various moral, social and religious matters as well. But while the law instructed God's people on *how* to worship God it did not actually *empower* them to worship God. It was basically a highly complex system of rules and regulations. Interestingly, no one was able to successfully or consistently keep the law of Moses. For example, God told His people in Deuteronomy 28 that if they would obey all of His commands they would be blessed with health, wealth and victory over their enemies all the days of their lives. But when we observe Israel's history we see there were many times that they suffered famines, disease and defeats in war. Why? Because no one was able to successfully and consistently keep and obey the law of Moses. However, the law did serve at least three functions:

1. It revealed how holy God is.
2. It revealed how weak and sinful humanity is.
3. It revealed the fact that we need a savior.

Remember, no one was able to consistently obey the entire law. It was an inadequate system of worship. God Himself knew this. So He promised that He would one day make a new covenant (New Testament) with His people:

**Behold, the days come; saith the LORD, that I will make a new covenant with the house of Israel, and with the house of Judah: Not according to the covenant that I made with their fathers in the day that I took them by the hand to bring them out of the land of Egypt; which my covenant they brake, although I was an husband unto them, saith the LORD: But this shall be the covenant that I will make with the house of Israel; after those days, saith the LORD, I will put my law in their inward parts, and write it in their hearts; and will be their God, and they shall be my people (Jeremiah 31:31-33).**

God desired a better covenant that would not be based only upon strict adherence to rules and regulations. He desired a much more intimate and personal relationship with His people. A relationship that would be founded and established on love. Love between Himself and humanity. He wanted one's obedience to be the result of one's love. And this would be the premise of the New Covenant. The prophet Ezekiel further prophesied this same point, only we find that Ezekiel's prophecy got a little more specific:

**A new heart also will I give you, and a new spirit will I put within you: and I will take away the stony heart out of your flesh, and I will give you an heart of flesh. And I will put my spirit within you, and cause you to walk in my statutes, and ye shall keep my judgments and do them (Ezekiel 36:26-27).**

This New Covenant initially involves God's Spirit literally dwelling within an individual. Fully and truly abiding in the New Covenant involves God's Spirit dwelling within. One is not fully and completely converted to God until God puts His Spirit within an individual and empowers them to do the things that are pleasing to God. The infilling or receiving of the Holy Ghost initiates one into the fullness of the New Covenant (New Testament). How can one consider himself to be a partaker of New Testament Christianity without receiving the *promise* of the New Testament? Again, it must be reiterated that this promise is not intended for only a select few Christians that God randomly chooses. It is the will of

God for every individual who considers himself to be a Christian to be filled with the Holy Ghost. Notice what Jesus said:

**He that believeth on me, as the scripture hath said, out of his belly shall flow rivers of living water. (But this spake he of the Spirit, which they that believe on him should receive: for the Holy Ghost was not yet given; should receive: for the Holy Ghost was not yet given; 39).**

If we believe on Jesus then we should receive the Holy Ghost. Notice also what Peter said concerning the infilling of the Holy Ghost:

**Then Peter said unto them, Repent, and be baptized every one of you in the name of Jesus Christ for the remission of sins, and ye shall receive the gift of the Holy Ghost. For the promise is unto you, and to your children, and to all that are afar off, even as many as the Lord our God shall call (Acts 2:38-39).**

Regardless of what popular opinion may be, the Apostle Peter said that the Holy Ghost is for all. Now this may surprise you, but did you know that one of the reasons Jesus died on the cross was so that we could finally be filled with the Spirit? Notice what Paul said:

**Christ hath redeemed us from the curse of the law, being made a curse for us: for it is written, Cursed is every one that hangeth on a tree: That the blessing of Abraham might come on the Gentiles through Jesus Christ; that we might receive the promise of the Spirit through faith (Galatians 3:13-14).**

The blood of Jesus that was shed on the cross cleanses us from our sins and grants us access to God. But that's not all it does. Jesus also died on the cross that we might receive the promise of the Spirit. Our relationship to God is incomplete without the infilling of the Holy Ghost.

In Matthew 3 and in Luke 3 John the Baptist also prophesied about the coming promise of the Holy Ghost:

**I indeed baptize you with water unto repentance: but he that cometh after me is mightier than I, whose shoes I am not worthy to bear: he shall baptize you with the Holy Ghost, and with fire (Matthew 3:11).**

In Acts 19 the Apostle Paul encountered some disciples of John the Baptist. He had to remind them (like so many need to be reminded today) of what John himself had said:

**He said unto them, Have ye received the Holy Ghost since ye believed? And they said unto him, We have not so much as heard whether there be any Holy Ghost. And he said unto them, Unto what then were ye baptized? And they said, Unto John's baptism. Then said Paul, John verily baptized with the baptism of repentance, saying unto the people, that they should believe on him which should come after him, that is, on Christ Jesus. When they heard this, they were baptized in the name of the Lord Jesus. And when Paul had laid his hands upon them, the Holy Ghost came on them; and they spake with tongues, and prophesied (Acts 19:2-6).**

Notice the two questions Paul had for these men:

1. How were you baptized?

2. Have ye received the Holy Ghost since ye believed?

There is nothing wrong with asking these same questions today to people who claim to be believing disciples. Maybe something's wrong if we're *not* asking. Before Paul left them, he made sure of two things:

1. They were baptized in the name of Jesus.
2. They received the Holy Ghost.

Why should we settle for any less today than what God has in store for us? In Romans 7 the Apostle Paul describes the weakness of our flesh because of that sin nature that lurks within every one of us. But in Romans 8 he describes the saving power of the Holy Spirit of God (*if* it be within us):

**So then they that are in the flesh cannot please God. But ye are not in the flesh, but in the Spirit, if so be that the Spirit of God dwell in you. Now if any man have not the Spirit of Christ, he is none of his. And if Christ be in you, the body is dead because of sin; but the Spirit is life because of**

**righteousness. But if the Spirit of him that raised up Jesus from the dead dwell in you, he that raised up Christ from the dead shall also quicken your mortal bodies by his Spirit that dwelleth in you (Romans 8:8-11).**

Apparently the hope of our salvation is contingent upon whether or not the Spirit of God dwells in us. Notice that there are four "if's" in the above passage of scripture indicating conditional phrases. Obviously we *need* the Spirit of God literally dwelling within us. Now please understand that it is a privilege to be filled with the Holy Ghost. It's not oppression. It's a blessing, not a burden. This is not bad news; it's good news. The promised availability of the Holy Ghost is still in existence today. Now please don't assume that one is automatically filled with the Holy Ghost at the moment of "believing" on Jesus Christ. Believing on Jesus is the first and primary prerequisite to Spirit baptism but it's not the ultimate and final objective. It's just the beginning. Notice the following passage:

**Then Philip went down to the city of Samaria, and preached Christ unto them. And the people with one accord gave heed unto those things which Philip spake, hearing and seeing the miracles**

which he did. For unclean spirits, crying with loud voice, came out of many that were possessed with them: and many taken with palsies, and that were lame, were healed. And there was great joy in that city. But there was a certain man, called Simon, which beforetime in the same city used sorcery, and bewitched the people of Samaria, giving out that himself was some great one: To whom they all gave heed, from the least to the greatest, saying, this man is the great power of God. And to him they had regard, because that of long time he had bewitched them with sorceries. But when they believed Philip preaching the things concerning the kingdom of God, and the name of Jesus Christ, they were baptized, both men and women. Then Simon himself believed also: and when he was baptized, he continued with Philip, and wondered, beholding the miracles and signs which were done. Now when the apostles which were at Jerusalem heard that Samaria had received the word of God, they sent unto them Peter and John: who, when they were come down, prayed for them, that they might receive the Holy Ghost: (For as yet he was fallen upon none of them: only they were baptized in the name of the Lord Jesus.) Then laid they their hands on them, and they received the Holy Ghost. And when Simon saw that through laying on of the

**apostles' hands the Holy Ghost was given, he offered them money, saying, Give me also this power, that on whomsoever I lay hands, he may receive the Holy Ghost (Acts 8:5-19).**

There are a couple of interesting facts worth pointing out in the above passage of scripture. First of all, just because the Samaritans believed in Jesus didn't mean that they were automatically filled with the Spirit. Peter and John came all the way to Samaria from Jerusalem specifically for the purpose of seeing that they would receive the Holy Ghost. Obviously there was yet more in store for these "believers." It is also very interesting to point out the fact that this man, Simon, was willing to pay money to have this power to fill people with the Holy Ghost. If imparting Spirit baptism consisted of merely instructing people to repeat the phrase "I accept the Lord Jesus Christ as my personal savior" why would Simon be willing to pay money to possess that power? Obviously something amazing and extraordinary occurred when an individual was filled with the Spirit. Also, if the Holy Ghost was automatically received at the moment of believing why did the Apostle Paul ask certain disciples, "Have ye received the Holy Ghost since ye believed?" (Acts 19:1-6).

I am of the persuasion that what was normal for the Book of Acts should be the norm for Christianity today. The Book of Acts is our role model or blueprint. It's the pattern of what the church should be today. When believers were filled with the Holy Ghost in the Book of Acts they spoke in tongues as the Spirit (Holy Ghost) gave the utterance.

**And they were all filled with the Holy Ghost, and began to speak with other tongues, as the Spirit gave the utterance (Acts 2:4).**

**While Peter yet spake these words, the Holy Ghost fell on all them which heard the word. And they of the circumcision which believed were astonished, as many as came with Peter, because that on the Gentiles also was poured out the gift of the Holy Ghost. For they heard them speak with tongues, and magnify God. Then answered Peter, Can any man forbid water, that these should not be baptized, which have received the Holy Ghost as well as we? (Acts 10:44-47).**

**And when Paul had laid his hands upon them, the Holy Ghost came on them; and they spake with tongues, and prophesied (Acts 19:6).**

Now according to the Apostle Paul, this particular phenomenon of speaking in tongues is intended to serve as a "sign" to unbelievers that they are without God. To understand this statement we must first go to the beginning. In Isaiah 28 we find that the Lord is prophesying against the people of Ephraim and Judah. In verse 2 it says that the Lord's mighty hand shall cast them down to the earth. In verse 7 it says that the priests and the prophets err through strong drink. The situation was so bad that even the priests and prophets (the moral teachers and leaders of the nation) were too drunk themselves to hear from God and offer sound judgment and direction to the people. In verse 8 it says that their tables were covered in vomit! This helps us to see the detestable condition that the nation had descended to.

In verse 9 God lamented the fact that He could not impart knowledge or direction unto them because they had become like infants (mentally). They were unable to perceive or comprehend His wisdom and guidance. God claimed that precept must be given upon precept and line upon line, here a little and there a little. But He couldn't get through to them as long as this tremendous "communication gap" existed. Much like an adult trying to have a meaningful conversation with an infant, His words were perceived as unintelligible senseless babble. So in verse 11 God declared in His judgment that He would yet get through to them. He claimed that with stammering lips and another tongue (language) He would speak to this people. Because of their sinfulness He was going to send them into foreign captivity, which was fulfilled in II Kings 17. As a form of judgment they would be taken captive and live as foreigners in a strange land. The foreign languages that would surround them would serve as a constant reminder or a sign that they were under the judgment of God. And so in I Corinthians 14:21 Paul made reference to this same incident and then stated, "Wherefore tongues are for a sign, not to them that believe, but to them that believe not." In other words, just as the foreign languages of the Assyrians served as a constant reminder or a sign to Ephraim and Judah that they were under the judgment of God, so too does speaking in tongues serve as a sign to unbelievers that they are without God. Again, our doctrine should not differ from that of the apostles. Are we so far removed from normal New Testament Christianity that normal New Testament Christianity actually seems *abnormal*? It's a sad period in Christendom when that becomes the case.

So according to the teachings of Jesus and His apostles, if an individual wants to be a full partaker of

New Testament Christianity, he or she needs to be filled with the Holy Ghost. If one truly desires the glory and power of God to abound within him he needs to be filled with the Holy Ghost. If one desires to emulate the ministry of Jesus Christ, he needs to be filled with the Holy Ghost. And if one wants to obey the Word of God, he needs to be filled with the Holy Ghost.

# Chapter Seven

## Seven Divine Coincidences

In the previous three chapters we encountered and examined three core doctrines that were consistently endorsed by Jesus and His apostles. They were the necessity of repentance, the necessity of water baptism and the necessity of Spirit baptism. Now it is very interesting to discover that these three components of a genuine conversion are contained and encapsulated in one brief passage of Scripture: Acts 2:38.

**Then Peter said unto them, Repent, and be baptized every one of you in the name of Jesus Christ for the remission of sins, and ye shall receive the gift of the Holy Ghost (Acts 2:38).**

By virtue of the fact that the teachings of John the Baptist, the disciples and the Lord Jesus Christ are once again reiterated and confirmed by none other than the apostle Peter in this one brief verse ought to render Acts 2:38 as one of the fundamental creeds of authentic Christianity. Acts 2:38 should never be considered as just some idle uttering to be casually disregarded and filed away in the archives of church history. No. It is in fact a treasure box of divine, soul-saving truths. Not only because it contains in a "capsule" form the teachings of Jesus and the apostles concerning salvation, and not only because it is a direct response to a direct question, "What shall we do [to be saved?]," but for several other reasons as well. The purpose of this chapter is to inform you of at least seven "back roads" that collectively and respectively lead the serious student of the New Testament back to Acts 2:38, thus reaffirming once again that Acts 2:38 is not some tired, worn-out cliché habitually quoted by uneducated nitwits. It is indeed a glistening jewel of colossal truth. Now because there may be some who will consider these seven reaffirming observations to be merely coincidences, for their sakes we will call this chapter Seven Divine "Coincidences."

**Coincidence #1:** In John 3:5 Jesus said "Except a man be born of water and of the Spirit, he cannot enter into the kingdom of God." When I ponder the words "cannot enter" certain images and phrases come to mind. Words like "no access," "closed" or "locked out." Sad, isn't it? Except a man be born of water and Spirit he cannot enter the kingdom. But what if someone were given keys to the kingdom? That would be wonderful, wouldn't it? Well, I've got good news for you. The Apostle Peter was granted the keys to the kingdom of heaven in Matthew 16:19. And in Acts 2:38 he declared what those keys are: repentance, baptism (water) and the infilling of the Holy Ghost (Spirit).Wow, what a coincidence!

**Coincidence #2:** In II Thessalonians 1:8 Paul said that Jesus would be revealed from heaven in flaming fire taking vengeance on them that obey not the gospel. In I Corinthians 15:1-4 Paul declared that the gospel consists of 3 things. They are the death, burial and resurrection of Jesus Christ. But how would one *obey* the gospel? Well, we obey the death when we obey the command to repent or "die" to our own self-will (Romans 6:11 and II Corinthians 5:15). We obey the burial when we obey the command to be "buried" in baptism (see Romans 6:3-5). We obey the resurrection when we obey the command to be filled with the Holy Ghost (born again of the Spirit) to walk in newness of life (Romans 8:8-11 and Ephesians 5:18). Hmmm, repentance, water baptism and Spirit baptism. Just like Acts 2:38. What a coincidence!

**Coincidence #3:** When the Apostle Paul encountered some partially converted disciples in Acts 19:1-6 he had two very important questions for them: "Have you received the Holy Ghost since you believed?" and "How were you baptized?" Before he left them he made sure that they were baptized in Jesus' name and had received the Holy Ghost. Just like Acts 2:38. Wow, what a coincidence!

**Coincidence #4:** The writer of Hebrews declared in Hebrews 6:1-2 that sincere Christians who truly desire to mature should all eventually move on past the basic "principles" of Christ and grow toward spiritual maturity. He then declares what those principles (basics, fundamentals) are. Interestingly they include "repentance" and the "doctrine of baptisms." The only baptisms I'm aware of that would qualify as principle doctrines would be water baptism and Spirit baptism. Amazingly these three "principles" are also commanded and endorsed by Peter in Acts 2:38. What a coincidence!

**Coincidence #5:** In Titus 3:5 Paul declared that we are not saved by works of righteousness (good deeds) but by the washing of regeneration (baptism) and renewing of the Holy Ghost. Again the same commands endorsed by Peter in Acts 2:38. What a coincidence!

**Coincidence #6:** In Acts 10 the Bible tells us about a man named Cornelius. According to the scriptures he was a devout man who feared God, gave money to the poor, and prayed often. Basically he lived a repented lifestyle. Sounds like a most certain candidate for heaven, right? But something was wrong. He still wasn't saved. So an angel appeared to Cornelius and instructed him to summons the Apostle Peter who would tell Cornelius what he ought to do to be saved (see Acts 10:1-6 and 11:14). Apparently in spite of all these wonderful character traits and good habits Cornelius still was not saved! Something was still missing! So Peter finally paid a visit to Cornelius and while Peter was expounding upon the person and power of Jesus Christ, suddenly Cornelius was filled with the Holy Ghost. Then immediately thereafter, Peter commanded (ordered, demanded) him to be baptized in the name of the Lord Jesus. Then Cornelius was saved! A devout (repented) man was filled with the Holy Ghost and baptized in Jesus' name. Wow, just like Acts 2:38! What a coincidence!

**Coincidence #7:** In Acts 8 the city of Samaria had gladly believed and received the things which Philip preached concerning Jesus. That's the first and primary prerequisite to salvation. Then after "believing" Philip they were baptized in the name of

Jesus (see Acts 8:12,16). Obviously Philip commanded them to be baptized. But something was still missing. So the apostles sent Peter and John to Samaria to pray for the people that they would receive the Holy Ghost. In Acts 8:17 they were filled with the Spirit. They repented, were baptized in the name of Jesus and filled with the Holy Ghost. The same things Peter endorsed and commanded in Acts 2:38. Wow, what a coincidence!

## A Final "Point" to Ponder

Land surveys are measured in degrees and minutes. A degree is 1/360 of a complete circle. A minute is 1/60 of a degree. If you were only one degree off from a point of reference in a 100-foot line you would find yourself nine inches away from your intended target at the other end of the line. If you were just one degree off from a point of reference in a ½ mile long line you would find yourself forty-six feet and one inch away from your intended target at the other end of the line. Just one degree off in a mile long line and you will find yourself ninety-two feet and two inches from your intended target at the other end of the line. From the earth to the moon, just one degree off from your point of reference and you will find yourself 2,160 miles away from your intended target!

Just one degree![1] The point is this: The New Testament church was founded upon the teachings of the Lord Jesus Christ and His apostles. The New Testament was finally completed and the last apostle died just before the end of the first century. It is in their writings that God has preserved and delivered to the human race the surest, most reliable and accurate point of reference. May we endeavor to never stray from it one degree or one minute. May we always endeavor to love, believe, embrace and obey it all the way to the other end of the line. Amen.

# Endnotes

**Chapter One**

1. Illustrations Unlimited, James S. Hewett (Tyndale House Publishers, Inc. Wheaton, Illinois) p. 321

**Chapter Two**

1. Ibid. p. 344
2. Speaker's Lifetime Library, Leonard and Thelma Spinard, (Prentice Hall Press, Paramus, New Jersey), p. 227

**Chapter Five**

1. The Baptismal Formula in Scripture and History, DKB, (Word Aflame Press, Hazelwood, Missouri)

**Chapter Seven**

1. These statistics were shared in a sermon delivered by Rev. Jon McDonald, Jr. in Stockton, CA. on January 25, 2000.

# Notes

# Notes

# Notes

# Notes

# Notes

21009322R00071

Made in the USA
Middletown, DE
16 June 2015